Father's Guide to Family Court

How I Represented Myself in Court - and WON!

C. T. SUMMERHAYES

Disclaimer:

(1)   Introduction to Disclaimer

This disclaimer governs the use of this book. By using this book, you accept this disclaimer in full with no exceptions.

(2)   No advice

The information contained herein does not constitute "legal advice", and should not be treated as such. The ideas, strategies, and tactics presented in this book are of a general nature, which may, or may not be applicable to your case.

You must not rely on the information herein as an alternative to legal advice. If you require legal advice, please consult a qualified professional.

You should never delay seeking legal advice because of the contents of this book.

(3)   No representations or warranties

The ideas, strategies, and tactics I present to you worked for me, but I cannot guarantee, nor do I claim that you will get the same results that I got.

To the maximum extent permitted by applicable law and subject to section 5 below, I exclude all representations, warranties, undertakings and guarantees relating to this book.

Without prejudice to the generality of the foregoing paragraph, I do not represent, warrant, undertake or guarantee:
* that the information in the book is correct, accurate, complete or non-misleading;
* that the use of the guidance in this book will lead to any particular outcome or result; or
* in particular, that by using the guidance in the book you will win your family court case.

(4)   Limitations and exclusions of liability

The limitations and exclusions of liability set out in this section and elsewhere in this disclaimer: are subject to section 6 below; and govern all liabilities arising under the disclaimer or in relation to this book, including liabilities arising in contract, in tort (including negligence) and for breach of statutory duty.

I will not be liable to you in respect of any losses arising out of any event or events beyond our reasonable control.
I will not be liable to you in respect of any business losses, including without limitation loss of or damage to profits, income, revenue, use, production, anticipated savings, business, contracts, commercial opportunities or goodwill.
I will not be liable to you in respect of any loss or corruption of any data, database or software.
I will not be liable to you in respect of any special, indirect or consequential loss or damage.

(5)   Exceptions

Nothing in this disclaimer shall: limit or exclude our liability for death or personal injury resulting from negligence; limit or exclude our liability for fraud or fraudulent misrepresentation; limit any of our liabilities in any way that is not permitted under applicable law; or exclude any of our liabilities that may not be excluded under applicable law.

(6)   Severability

If a section of this disclaimer is determined by any court or other competent authority to be unlawful and/or unenforceable, the other sections of this disclaimer continue to be in effect.

If any unlawful and/or unenforceable section would be lawful or enforceable if part of it were deleted, that part will be deemed to be deleted, and the rest of the section will continue in effect.

(7)   Responsibility

You are fully and solely responsible under all circumstances for any course of action you take in your family law matter.

I will not be held responsible for any loss or damage incurred by the application of any principles, strategies, tips and/or advice presented herein.

Although I do have a track record of success in family court, I have not been formally educated in family law. Use the information provided herein at your own risk.

(8)   Our details

In this disclaimer, "I" means the author of this book, C. T. Summerhayes.

Table of Contents

Prologue

Court battles are exhausting. They can exhaust your patience, emotions, and most of all - your finances. Most fathers simply do not have the resources to pay a lawyer all the way through court, which can include a lengthy trial. Legal fees can be overwhelming. Most fathers are not aware that legal fees can exceed the cost of buying a home.

Unfortunately, many fathers give up, or give in because they don't have the resources to continue. Their bank accounts are drained. Their energy is drained. Their emotions are spent. They feel like they are at the end of their rope. Many fathers end up reluctantly agreeing to something they do not think is right or fair.

Many fathers give up, not only because they run out of money, but because they do not know how to effectively represent themselves in court. The thought of going through a trial without a lawyer can be very intimidating, but it doesn't have to be.

With education, aptitude, and the right attitude you can win!

How I Represented Myself in Court - and WON!!!

Background

It was 2006. After being married for almost 10 years at this point, things have deteriorated to the point where we just couldn't stand each other.

But this didn't happen overnight. In fact, the marriage started to dissolve within weeks of the wedding. There were numerous times that we nearly left each other. But neither marriage, nor divorce was something that I took lightly. Thus I stuck it out for nearly 10 years. If it wasn't for my moral convictions it would have been over long before that.

Nonetheless, in 2004 my son, Elijah, was born. But things didn't get any better. Tension within the marriage was at an all time high. I don't deem it appropriate to publicly diss my ex (whom I will call "Sue"), but there were a lot of things going on behind the scenes. It became very apparent that divorce was on the horizon. But who would have custody of Elijah?

Recognizing the state the marriage was in, I finally decided to find a "good" family law lawyer. I called many lawyers in the area. I was looking for someone that I "click" with... someone who knew their stuff in court... someone that I could trust.

I had a long list of reasons why I believed that my son, Elijah, needed to be in my custody. I thought that since I had a full-time job, the child would be better off with me, because I made the money. My ex had a part-time job. Being somewhat naive, it didn't dawn on me that I would ever have to pay support.

I didn't have any past exposure to family court, divorce, and custody issues. I made a lot of assumptions regarding family law. I didn't know anyone personally that had been through the system. I was quite uninformed about the "game".

I made the same mistake that many fathers do - I assumed that the family court system would just hear me out, and see that I was the best candidate for custody.

There were many reasons for me to win. Besides, I had a great relationship with my son! I already was the primary caregiver in his life. I made all the decisions. I always led the way in the family. I was the one who decided to take him to the doctor when he was sick. I changed his diapers and bathed him most of the time. I was the one who first taught him how to eat with utensils. I was the one who helped him take his first step. His mother was not there many evenings. She worked evenings, and she always got up late (noon).

I believed that I was clearly the best choice if there ever was a choice to be made as far as who should have custody. I just assumed that the facts were obvious. And I believed that any family court judge would judge accordingly.

As soon as Sue got wind of my lawyer consultations she suddenly tried to spend more time with him. Tension in the home was very high. Things eventually escalated. I needed to make a choice: to proceed with legal separation and divorce, or not to.

The Decision to Proceed With Lawyer #1 - Brian

After making many phone calls, and talking to many lawyers, I finally found one who seemed to be the best. I will call him "Brian". Brian spent lots of time talking to me on the phone. He was easy to talk to, and seemed to know his stuff. He had a string of degrees behind his name and he was relatively inexpensive.

Finally, I thought, I found a good lawyer. He was educated, professional, and easy to talk to. I liked him.

After much deliberating, I decided to begin the legal process. Brian told me that as the applicant (plaintiff) I will have an "edge" on the case. So I decided to initiate the process. Even though I hired Brian, I was always open for second opinions. I consulted many lawyers which gave me lots of advice. Most of the lawyers I spoke to said that I have at least 70% chance of winning custody.

In fact at one time I travelled over 100 km just to sit down with a lawyer for advice. He was very expensive. After everything was said and done, his advice wasn't of much help. But he also told me that I have a good chance of winning custody. I was desperate for all the advice I could get.

First Court Appearance

After the initial court documents were filed, the first court hearing was scheduled. I attended with my lawyer, Brian. And my ex attended with her lawyer. Just before we were scheduled to go in, her lawyer called Brian to the side and had a "chat". Then Brian came to me and explained that the other party is going to ask for a mutual non-harassment order seeing that we were still living in the same house.

I wasn't sure what to say, but I trusted that Brian knew what he was doing. The first time before the judge, we were seated to his (the judge's) right-hand side in front of the bench. They had to call the other party over the intercom because they were not there. Both Sue and her lawyer came in walking down the aisle hand-in-hand. At that point I could easily see how her lawyer was quite a show! He might as well have kissed her in front of the judge!

Nevertheless, court was in order. And of course, at my first appearance I wanted to make a good impression to the judge. But regardless of the fact that I was the applicant (plaintiff) in this case, her lawyer was the first to talk. In fact, he did almost all of the talking. My lawyer only said yes, or no to questions that were asked. Immediately after that meeting I felt degraded. Not only because the opposing lawyer did all of the talking. But it was the way he spoke. He made me look like the bad guy, and my lawyer said little to nothing in response.

Without any reason whatsoever he asked the judge for a mutual non-harassment order, making me look like I had been harassing her. This was agreed upon without any evidence of harassment whatsoever. There were no allegations of harassment. I realise that may be normal for couples living together and going through a divorce. But I didn't feel like it was necessary. And later I regretted agreeing to it. It made me look like I was prone to harass her, which wasn't the case.

I wasn't very happy with how Brian handled the hearing. He let the other party do all the talking. In my opinion, he certainly did not do a very good job. I called him after the fact and let him know what I thought. He assured me that regardless of the seemingly bad impression in court things will work out for me.

As time went on I began to get more and more frustrated with Brian. He didn't return calls in a timely fashion. Sometimes I had to call him multiple times before he returned my call.

I was away one weekend. When I got back, my ex was in the front yard. When she saw me coming she ran to the neighbors house and told me that if I went in the house she would call the police. I was always told to do everything you can to avoid conflict. So I thought I would be wise to leave and call my lawyer and ask for advice.

Brian advised me to stay away from the house, considering how volatile things were. He said that it would be the wisest thing to do seeing that she could make things much worse by calling the police and making false accusations. And staying away from the house could potentially keep me out of jail. Seeing that he had experience and education in these kind of matters I took his advice. I stayed away.

This caused me great pain as I didn't get to see my son. The more and more time went by, the more I realized that I wouldn't be able to see my son for an indefinite period of time. This took a toll on me, and I believe that this also took a toll on my son because he was so used to being with me.

Several weeks passed. I was speaking to Brian on the telephone when he mentioned that he got a letter from the other party containing an affidavit from a family member - against me! I asked him when he received it. Brian told me that he received it weeks ago.

It took weeks for him to tell me of this affidavit against me? I had enough. This is when I decided to look for another lawyer. I didn't feel he did a good job in court, and his timing and organizational skills were not the best. This is not to mention the phone calls not returned in a timely fashion, or not returned at all.

I started calling around again, "shopping" for another lawyer.

Lawyer #2 - Ted

I came across another lawyer, whom I will call "Ted" who seemed to be a lot better. When I first spoke to him I told him that I was shopping for a good lawyer, and I asked him straight out why I should hire him over any other lawyer.

He told me of his 25+ years of experience in family court, his good standing with legal organizations, and his trustworthy character. I briefly told him about the experiences I had with Brian. He assured me that he would never let a call go without reply, and in a timely fashion. He said that his policy is to always return calls, or emails within 24 hours.

Looking back, I must say that he did live up to that promise. He always returned calls and emails within 24 hours. I was very pleased with that.

Ted came across like a lion. He seemed very aggressive. This is what I was looking for in a lawyer. I wanted someone to go in and "fight" for me. I wanted someone to go it and tear apart the opposition.

I'm not sure why, but Ted seemed to change his tune over time. He went from singing a song of victory to singing a song of concession.

It all culminated one day as I spent 1 hour arguing with Ted on the phone. I told him all the reasons why I thought I should have sole custody of my son. And these reasons were quite legitimate. But Ted told me that as a father I have an uphill battle. He said that it is nearly impossible for a father to obtain sole custody unless there is a "life and death" situation, or unless the mother is obviously unfit with plenty of evidence to prove that.

If the mother is a serious drug addict, or is never at home, and neglects or endangers the child with plenty of evidence to prove it - then, according to Ted I would have a good chance of getting full custody - otherwise I would not.

During that hour-long argument I had with Ted I told him that I would still like to continue to fight. Then he told me that, with his experience, he doesn't think I have a chance at winning custody - not even joint custody. He told me that if I lose I would have to pay not only his fees, but also the fees of the other party.

Finally, after an hour of arguing with him, he convinced me to surrender all custody to my ex. I did so very reluctantly because I knew it wasn't the best for the child. However, I trusted my lawyer who said I didn't have much of a choice. I felt like I had to give in to a system that I was powerless to change - Although it desperately needed changing because it did not provide justice for my family.

The next few years proved to be that of much horror. My ex moved with my son to a city 1.5 hours drive (on a good day) from where I live. I had to pay spousal support, child support, plus travel expenses to see my son. This claimed at least half of my take home pay. I had to live on credit cards and loans from the bank. Eventually, every credit limit was exhausted.

The ruthless grip I was under caused me to descend into a downward spiral financially that eventually caused me to cash in all my RRSP's just to pay the bills. Ultimately I had to file for personal bankruptcy.

The bankruptcy trustee told me that he is seeing more and more fathers who are in the same position: forced to file for bankruptcy protection due to high support payments.

Who pays for this? Everybody does.

Faith

I would be doing you a great injustice if I were to fail to mention my faith as a key factor in my success. During the whole legal process, I continued to pray and seek His guidance. I consider His guidance and influence to be essential for my overall well being.

Having said that, I believe that God was with me through the whole ordeal. The stress was very great at times. Yet I never turned to any kind of drug. I never turned to alcohol for relief. Rather, I turned to the God whom I know.

Please note: It is an asset to find a good faith community for support. Also, getting your child involved in a faith community is a great addition to the list of why the child benefits from his or her relationship with you.

The Turning Point

In 2008, Sue became friends with one of my old friends. This proved to be an invaluable asset. While talking on the phone one day, I briefly told Sue of my financial woes. She told me that she is willing to terminate spousal support.

I knew that I had to jump on the opportunity before she changed her mind, as she so frequently did. I called the local courthouse, and found out what forms I needed to to fill out in order to initiate the process. After completing the forms I had to find a witness. It happened to be that my old friend, who was a mutual friend with Sue, needed a ride to town. I gave him a ride to town on the day that I was supposed to meet my ex to review the documents.

On the way, I explained to him what Sue said. I told him I have some paperwork to sign and I asked him if he wouldn't mind being a witness for me. He agreed.

We all met at a donut shop. Just before signing the documents, my ex suddenly wasn't "sure" anymore. I reminded her of her promise to terminate the spousal support. My friend encouraged her to sign the papers telling her that it is much easier to settle out of court. She agreed and signed. I then went through the necessary measures to make sure the consent motion was made into a court order.

Hope

The termination of spousal support was the first ray of hope I saw in getting out of the horrible financial condition I was in.

But, in spite of the termination of spousal support my financial condition was still spiralling out of control headed for a crash. This was due to the fact that the support payments were so high that it drove me deep in debt.

The debt was so great that I couldn't even keep up to the minimum payments let alone the interest that accumulated on top of that. I managed to control the snowball effect of interest by negotiating with my creditors. But it was too late. I was too far in debt. My family came first. That meant, for the most part, that the payments made toward a mountain of debt were very little.

At that point in my life I was married with three children. My wife, and I tried our best to live off of as little as possible as we tried to whittle down the debt. But all of our efforts were to no avail.

Calls were pouring in from collection agencies to the point of harassment. We started getting letters from lawyers threatening legal action. In fact a lawyer called a few times personally.

It was at this point we realized that we were in a nose dive for rock bottom. In our desperation to find solutions we ultimately ran across a bankruptcy trustee. I certainly didn't want to file for bankruptcy. I did everything in my power to avoid it. But the bills kept coming in. The harassing calls grew in frequency and severity. We started getting letters from lawyers. The letters and calls from lawyers pushed us to the point of saying a) its either we are going to get dragged into court or b) we file bankruptcy.

I consulted several people for advice before making any decisions. At last, I contacted my pastor. He told me that he knew of people who filed for bankruptcy protection. He said that it was like being "born again" financially, and that it was an opportunity to find grace in the legal system.

After consulting several people, including my pastor, I finally decided to file for bankruptcy protection.

Back to Court

It was in the spring of 2009 when my ex broke the news to me: she was going to move to back to Toronto. I immediately tried to talk her out of it. I knew that if she moved to Toronto my family would be finished. I wouldn't be able to see Elijah very often. Due to my financial condition I couldn't afford to drive all the way to Toronto on a regular basis. When Elijah lived in Toronto in 2007 it cost me almost a weeks pay in gas alone per month. And with the gasoline now more expensive, it would only be worse.

I knew I had to do something. Its either a) let Elijah move to Toronto, which is not in his best interest. Besides such a move could cause my family to fall apart, or b) go back to court.

With my initial step in representing myself in the mutual consent motion terminating spousal support I kind of got my feet wet, so to speak. I knew I couldn't afford a lawyer and the court wouldn't allow me to obtain a subsidized lawyer. Therefore, I was forced to initiate the whole court process myself.

Fortunately, my employer offered a program called EAP (Employee Assistance Program) that allowed me to obtain free legal advice over the telephone through their EAP lawyers.
At this point I was willing to take every little bit of help that I could get. In fact, I sought as much help as possible. I asked around as much as possible. I spoke to the clerks at the court. I called every helpline I could find. And I scoured the Internet for help.

I quickly began to realize that help was not easy to find without money. However, I obtained a good deal of help from information I could gather from free lawyer consultations, the Internet, court clerks, and my EAP.

Learning court procedure was a challenge. I found out that the courts do not work the way I thought they would. You can't just walk into court and say, "Here I am! Listen to my story." There are certain steps, and procedures to go through. And you must do it in the proper way.

Upon the advice of the EAP lawyers I filed an emergency motion seeing that she could take off at any time for Toronto. I filed the appropriate documents at court and then I served her.

The emergency motion hearing came to pass and I had a chance to present the case to the judge. I didn't get a chance to say much other than the reason for filing an emergency motion.

During an emergency motion only one party is present before the judge. This is due to the possibility that if the other party finds out before the court date they may kidnap the child.

The judge asked why I wasn't represented. I told him that I didn't have the money to hire a lawyer. The judge then asked one of the court reporters to call a specific lawyer who represented another case previous to mine on that same day, hoping that he was still in the building. The reporter called that lawyer through the P.A. system.

In a matter of seconds the lawyer responded, and came into the courtroom. The judge asked him to do a "favor for the court" and represent me for this emergency motion. I sat down with the lawyer for a few minutes and briefly explained the scenario to him. He suggested that we ask the judge to make an order to restrict the child from being taken out of the county for any longer than 12 hours at any given time.

I agreed, and we went before the judge. The lawyer explained to the judge that since the last court order many things have happened. Because of a history of taking the child away for indefinite periods of time, without my knowledge, we asked that there would be an order put in place to restrict the child from being taken out of the county for any more than 12 hours.

I spoke up and asked for police enforcement. This I asked because I know by experience that the police will not assist you in enforcing a family court order without a court order including police enforcement.

The judge agreed.

The judge ordered that the child is not to be taken out of the county for any more than 12 hours at a time except for medical reasons. He also endorsed police enforcement, and that we are both to attend court again in 8 days to initiate court proceedings with the other party!

I immediately obtained a court order solidifying the judge's endorsement.

I served the court order on my ex.
She hired the same lawyer that she had last time through court. I knew from last time that he (her lawyer) is very aggressive.

Eight days later we were back in court. This time I had to face my ex with her lawyer.

After her lawyer had his say, the judge overrode the emergency order and changed the 12 hour restraint to 48 hours. We also set a date for a case conference, starting the process which could eventually end up to be a full-blown trial.

Throughout this process I received a lot of letters and court documents from the other party that was quite inflammatory, and upsetting as much of what was said was absolutely untrue. And her lawyer pushed the limits far beyond reason. However, I was warned by other lawyers that this is normal and is to be expected.

One day, while being "on the street" outside of an apartment building one gentleman told me that my ex would win, and that she had all the documentation to prove it. Apparently, Sue was proudly spreading the message that she was going to win. I had a couple of people who told me that I am not doing the right thing.

Another person tried to discourage me from following through with the court battle, saying that I was "opening a can of worms" that I shouldn't get into. I was told that I would end up in a worse state in the long run.

But I couldn't leave it alone. I couldn't let things go. Leaving it alone, and not initiating a court battle would mean that I would risk losing my son, and not being able to see him much at all. I knew that it was in the child's best interest to be with me. This is not to mention many other problems that amount to the fact that if I were to leave it alone, it would not be in my son's best interest.

If I didn't go back to court, I would not be able to see my son. I was simply too far in debt, and due to my financial condition, I could not afford travel expenses to see my son. Besides that, my financial condition was a direct result of steep support payments.

High support payments would have a snowball effect on my relationship with my son. Not only could I not afford to see him often. But even when I did have time with him, the quality of our relationship would be compromised because of the immense financial stress in my life.

This indeed spilled over into every part of my life. At work I wasn't able to perform as well due to stress. At home I wasn't able to enjoy relationships with family and friends as well as I should have for the same reason.

The steps I had to go through in court are as follows: file a motion with supporting affidavit, motion hearing, case conference, settlement conference, trial management conference, and ultimately, trial. Please keep in mind that these steps may or may not be applicable in your area.

You don't have to go through all those steps. If you can settle out of court, you are opted out. This can happen at any stage. For example, if you come to an agreement halfway through the process (i.e. settlement conference) then the court proceedings will go no further, and a court order will be issued. However, if you cannot come to an agreement, you can expect to go to trial.

After receiving numerous letters from her lawyer, most of which were filled with inaccuracies, and unreasonable requests, we proceeded through to the settlement conference.

Based on the advice of my EAP lawyers, I asked for the settlement conference and the trial management conference to be combined. This saves a lot of time and money.

During the settlement conference, I paid close attention to what Sue's lawyer had to say. I wanted to prepare myself for his arguments. Once I know the arguments, I can properly prepare a counter-argument. That way, I am not taken "off guard".

It became very evident at the settlement conference that neither I, nor my ex was willing to budge on a single point. I asked the court for sole custody. She was not willing to negotiate.

The decision was made to proceed to trial.

Knowing that my case was going to trial presented quite a challenge. After all, I was self-represented. The only advice I got was from the EAP lawyers, and whatever I could scrape up on the Internet. I tried to find any kind of free legal help I could get. But it was very scarce.

I started to educate myself as to what a trial consisted of. I found out that the applicant (plaintiff) is responsible for producing the trial record, an opening statement, direct examination, cross examination, and a closing statement.

But one of the most valuable things anyone can do, representing yourself, or not, is to go to court and sit in on another case that is similar to yours.

I called the court and asked if there were any family court trials coming up. The Trial Coordinator gave me a date of a family trial that was scheduled before my trial commenced.

So I went, properly dressed, with a pen (and a spare) and a notepad to record the entire thing.
I sat there and took notes on everything. This proved to be a tremendous source of education. I learned what to do, and what not to do. I learned from other people's mistakes. This gave me a good idea of how things went, and how a family trial is handled in court. It was a great example because the applicant for that trial was self represented, and the respondent had a lawyer - just like my case.

After the trial was done I went through my notes reliving the trial so that I could have it engraved on my mind. I didn't want to forget anything. I learned a lot by this experience.

Based upon that experience, coupled with the advice I was able to glean off of the Internet, I drafted the entire trial from opening statement to closing statement.

I spent a lot of time preparing. I took a lot of time off of work to prepare the documents. I attended every father's support group meeting I could. I continued to seek help until the day came.

Trial

The day of the trial finally came. All the way down to the courthouse, which was about a half an hour drive, I was praying fervently for help. After all, if I didn't get God's help then it would be only little ol' me against an experienced lawyer. But if I could be granted grace and honor from heaven, then nothing could stop me. I desperately needed God's help, and I knew it.

I remember reading on the Internet about someone who represented themselves, and started their opening statement by apologizing for being self-represented. So I decided that is how I would start as well.

A three day trial was scheduled in April of 2010. At the end of the 2nd day, Sue's lawyer said that he had to go on a vacation in Florida.

Perhaps he had the feeling that he was losing and he needed more time to prepare. However, the judge suspended the trial for 2 months.
I was a little apprehensive of this because I didn't want it to be put off too long. I thought that the other party was just playing the game of putting things off.

Anyway, it wasn't put off too long. And it gave me a chance to prepare more too. Having a two month break two thirds of the way through trial gave me a chance to review everything - especially my cross examination, and closing statement, as we didn't get that far yet. For this reason the break actually worked out in my favor.

During my two month break I scripted my cross examination, and closing statement. I was able to take the information I got in the first two days of trial to help me form the best cross-examination. I actually needed this extra time anyway because I wasn't fully prepared for the last half of the trial.

The first two days of the trial included opening statements from both parties, my testimony, cross examination of me, direct and cross examinations of all of my witnesses (three witnesses in total).

When the last day of the trial came in June I was completely prepared. I knew what was in store. My ex had to be interviewed by her attorney, and I had to cross examine her. Also, her witness told her side of the story, and I also cross examined her. The day ended with a closing statement from both myself and the other party.

The judge exercised "reserved judgement", which means that the "verdict" or results of the trial would be withheld until an unknown date, when the judge will finally give the judgment.

I was told that the results of the trial, or the "judgment" can take up to 18 months in some cases. In my case it only took a few months as the judge promised to have it in before the beginning of the next school year so that we can properly prepare.

I will never forget the day that I received a call from the court saying that the judgement is in. At the time I was home with my wife and 3 children. As soon as I received the call I ran down to the courthouse.

I went to the clerk's office and they told me to go upstairs to the trial coordinator's office. I went upstairs and knocked on the door. She answered and told me that I have to wait until she gets it all ready, which didn't take very long. She told me that she cannot give me the judgement earlier than she gives the other party. She faxed the entire judgement (9 pages) to my ex's attorney's office. Immediately after the fax went through she gave me a copy of the judgment.

I took it and thanked her, and left. On the way home I read the judgement. I will never forget the feeling. My prayers have been answered. I was given sole custody, and my arrears have been completely forgiven. I have never felt so grateful in all my life. I wouldn't have been happier if I won a billion dollars! I could hardly contain myself.

Practical Guide

This guide is written primarily with the self-represented father in mind, as most fathers are either self-represented, or will be, due to the enormous legal fees that are incurred through a lengthy court battle.

Even if you have a lawyer, you need to know these things. Remember, you are the boss. In order to be an effective boss, you must know "the ropes". The lawyer serves you, not vise-versa. You need to be educated as much as possible to effectively take charge of your case.

Be a Good Father

This book is written with the assumption that you are a "decent" father. Fathers who struggle with lifestyle issues, substance abuse, or behavioral issues need to deal with those problems **before** ever attempting to gain custody of their child.

If you presently have issues with alcohol abuse, drug use, anger, fits of rage, violence, or anything else that would impede your ability to be a decent father, you need to deal with that first. Seek help. Be proactive seeking help. Make sure you get documents to prove you are currently seeking help. You must prove to the judge that you are serious, and that sufficient progress has been made to better yourself.

Keep in mind that you don't have to be "perfect". But, if you struggle with any of these kind of issues, you should take the necessary steps to deal with it.

Why Do Children Need Their Fathers

There is a "famine" of real fathers in the land. When I say "father" here, I am not talking about a biological male who plays a part in the conception of a child. I am talking about a real father, who knows how to "father" his children - a father who is a responsible, reliable, mature, loving, and a secure leader in the family.

Many homes are single parent homes. Many fathers are absent. "Fatherhood" has become a dirty word. The presence of fathers, who truly "father" their children are rare. To be truly fathered is the greatest need of modern society, and it is the cry of this generation. Masculinity needs to make a great comeback. And in fact, masculinity will make a comeback. The revival of masculinity, and good fatherhood starts at home - with you!

For millennia, the father was the center of the family. Things have not gotten any better. In fact, things have gotten worse for the true lifeblood of society - the traditional nuclear family, of which the father is the cornerstone.

It is said that in prisons, on Mother's Day, a lot of Mother's Day cards are sold. But the celebration of Father's Day is almost non-existent. Not very many Father's Day cards are sold to prison inmates.

The absence of true, loving, masculine fathers has taken it's toll. Our society needs fathers!

First Things First

If you are facing criminal charges, make sure that you get that out of the way before family court. Make that your priority. This is crucial as the outcome of Criminal Court can directly affect the outcome of Family Court. Do everything you can to ensure that your criminal case goes through court as fast as possible. Time away from your child is not good under any circumstance.

Note: Criminal court and criminal law is not the theme of this book. However, some of the principles covered herein can be also be useful in criminal court.

Preparation is Key

Don't think you can just walk into court and say, "Hi. I'm dad. Hear my story!"

In order to win your case, you need to be well educated, and well prepared. This will require time and skill. It takes time to study, prepare court documents, and write your testimony. If you don't "have" time, you must make time.

In my experience, I had to take time off work to do this. Personally, I took several weeks off of work to study and prepare. I didn't take all the time off at once. Sometimes I took a day off, and sometimes I took several days off. Either way, you **must** make time.

Don't become family court roadkill! You need to prepare. You need to prepare your evidence. But more than that, you need to prepare yourself.

Prepare a defence whenever possible. Make sure you write it down!

Keep Your Child First

Preparation, and education can take a great deal of time, but make sure it doesn't take time away from you and your child. If you are separated from your child(ren), you need to do whatever it takes to ensure the child knows that you have not forgotten him, or her.

Some of you do not have contact with your child. So this can be difficult, but not impossible. You can let them know you care in more ways than one. Even in the worst-case-scenario, you can do whatever it takes to let them hear "through the grapevine" that you are trying to contact them.

For those of you who have contact with your children, making sure they know you haven't forgotten them involves much more than just words. Don't just call your child and say, "I have not forgotten you". Rather, do what you can to spend some quality time with your child. Do something special with them. Treat them to something special.

It could be as simple as spending some quality time on the phone talking with your child. Take time to listen to what they have to say. Make a good conversation.

But preferably, whenever possible, quality time should be spent in person. Do something they love to do.

Take time. And as usual, always document.

Don't Be Too Nice!

Do you suffer from the "White Knight Syndrome"?
If so, you may be snatching defeat out of the jaws of victory! Being too nice can be your downfall.

Some men have not yet accepted the fact that she made the decision to separate. He is focussed on saving the marriage. He has not accepted that she is finished. He assumes that she really doesn't mean it, and he continues to smother her in love.

He thinks that he just needs to romance her. But all he does is bury his head in the sand.

Don't lose objectivity. Don't lose objective reality.

You may have to accept the fact that that she is done!

Don't be too nice. She'll use what she can to get what she wants and then turn on you!

The 7 Nevers

When things go wrong:

1. NEVER leave the home. It gives the other party de facto custody. Even leaving for a few days can give the other party de facto custody. You could easily lose your children by simply leaving the home.
2. NEVER let your emotions get out of control.
3. NEVER threaten to hurt anyone.
4. NEVER assault anyone under any circumstance.
5. NEVER practice parental alienation. Do not alienate your child from their mother unless you can prove beyond all doubt that doing so is in the best interest of the child. Even in bad circumstances, at least telephone access is usually granted. Be reasonable.
6. NEVER give up your right to be a parent. Do not ever surrender your privilege and responsibility to parent your child.
7. NEVER leave everything into the hands of your lawyer. Your lawyer works for you - not the other way around. You need to be informed, and educated. Be proactive! Get educated!

7 Things You NEED to Know

1. the rules of the court;
2. court procedures;
3. the law that applies to your case;
4. the evidence you need to prove your case;
5. how to write affidavits, and complete court forms;
6. how to argue effectively; and
7. what will happen if you win, or lose your case.

You don't have to know all these at the very beginning, but as time goes on you must learn these things. Whatever the case, learn them before your trial.

Hiring a Lawyer

Most people who go through a family court trial end up with either an enormous legal bill, or they are forced to go through the process without a lawyer because they cannot afford one. I am not saying a lawyer shouldn't be involved, but many fathers cannot afford it.

If you have the financial resources to hire a lawyer you must make full use of both your time and the lawyer's time while represented. In other words, when you have a lawyer at your disposal, make the most of the time you have with that lawyer because you may not have him/her very long.

Dedicate an enormous amount of time thinking about questions to ask the lawyer beforehand. Find someone who you can trust to talk to, and brainstorm with. Take your time. This kind of thing cannot be rushed. And make sure that you write all your questions down. Make sure you carry a cell phone or other device to record the questions, or buy a small pocket-size notepad, and a pen to carry with you at all times. You don't want to think of a great question, only to forget it because you didn't write it down!

Give it a matter of several days because sometimes things can temporarily slip from your mind. And sometimes, over a course of several days, other things arise that bring more questions. And perhaps you can get some of your questions answered using the resources available to you on the Internet.

However you do it, make sure that you have a list a questions to ask your lawyer while you have his/her time.

Remember, unless you are fairly wealthy, you probably won't have that lawyer very long. It is easy to blow a whole year's pay in a matter of a few weeks with a lawyer.

Find a lawyer that specifically deals with family court, not criminal court. If you have a criminal matter in the courts too, then it would be best to get a separate lawyer for criminal court.

Get a Lawyer Who is Good Representing Fathers

Family matters are serious matters. Don't just settle for a "generic" lawyer for the job. Don't hire just any lawyer.

Ask your lawyer if he/she has experience representing fathers in court. If so, you need to ask how many fathers they represented actually won custody.

Very important: Once you find a lawyer who says that he/she had success in family court representing fathers the next thing you should say is, "Show me the court orders."

You need a lawyer who can prove to you that he, or she is good at representing fathers. Anyone can represent a mother and win. Generally speaking, it is easy representing a mother. But you need a lawyer that is specifically good with fathers. If you are going to be investing your hard-earned money into this lawyer you need to ask him/her to prove himself by showing you court orders of cases they fought where the father won!

Remember, lawyers should be used to proving things. You need to see several final court orders. Don't settle for just one order. And don't be afraid to ask.

When the lawyer shows you court orders, make sure the order is a final order, not a temporary order. It should clearly say "Final Order".

Make sure it is not an order that was made on consent. An order that is made on consent simply means that the order was agreed to by both parties without a fight. It takes little, to no skill on the lawyers part to be a part of an order that was made on consent.

If the lawyer gives you a hard time, assure him/her that you don't need to see names - just proof that he/she has represented fathers and won. If they come up with an excuse saying that they can't reveal personal details about their clients, <u>ask them to black out the names!</u>

Bottom line: you need proof. If a lawyer is not able to produce court orders where they fought for a father and won, then they probably don't have one. Move on... find another lawyer.

Finding a lawyer *for fathers* is not easy. It may take a lot of searching, but they are out there. Don't settle for anything less.

Good Talker?

Don't judge a lawyer by his mouth. In other words, he/she may be a great "talker". He, or she may be very aggressive. This can be impressive. But the judge may not be impressed. Judges are used to "the game". They can see through the empty words.

Highly Paid?

Also, do not judge a lawyer by his bill. A lawyer who charges more is not always a better lawyer than the others. Judge a lawyer by his or her success, <u>proven</u> by court orders of cases where they successfully represented fathers.

Final Thoughts on Hiring a Lawyer...

Finally, <u>don't hire a lawyer that is a friend of the other party's lawyer!</u>

And <u>never</u> hire a lawyer who represents both parties.

Employer Assistance Programs

Some employers offer EAPs that include <u>free legal advice</u>. Check with your employer's Human Resource Department to see if they offer "Employer Assistance Programs". This can be a priceless asset.

Call your EAP lawyer as much as you can. Don't be afraid to ask for help when you need it. Knowing that you need help is half the battle.

Free Consultations

Get a list of lawyers in your area and call around. Be honest, tell the lawyer that you are "shopping" for a good lawyer. Ask them if they offer free initial consultations. Many do. Sometimes they will give you a free initial telephone consultation the first time you call.

Be prepared. Think ahead before calling a lawyer. Think of all the questions you want to ask. Be ready in case they take your questions the first time you call!

Think about all the "what ifs". Think as far ahead as possible. Ask as many questions as possible during your allotted free consultation. Make sure you write all the questions down.

Remember, you are "on the clock". The lawyer is not going to give you all the time in the world in your free consultation. Make the best of it.

What About Mediation?

Mediation is when you sit down with a mediator and try to come to a "happy-medium" between you and your ex-wife. A mediator then strikes a balance and makes a deal.

But be careful with a mediator. If you don't do your homework and find out everything there is to find out about that mediator beforehand you can be in a very bad place.

In Court

I do not recommend that you go to court, and tell the judge why the world needs fathers. That won't work. Court is not a place to argue about society's issues. Rather, you must sell yourself as the best candidate for custody of your child.

Produce practical evidence showing how you benefit your child's life. More than that - give evidence proving that you are a vital element in the child's life. This should not only include playing games with your children, but also taking time to help your child complete his, or her homework, helping your child get better grades, and bonding with them in deep and meaningful ways.

It's Your Attitude, Not Your Aptitude

Years ago I was hunting for a good paying job. I decided to look in the newspaper classifieds. A job caught my eye which offered good pay: Sales agent for a third-party natural gas reseller. I decided to make the call.

The lady that I was speaking with gave me directions to the office for a meeting. It was located in another city, but I was willing to make the commute.

When I got there I noticed it wasn't a personal job interview, as I originally thought. Rather, it was a training session for those interested. The room was filled with about 20+ people. They taught us "the ropes" in selling natural gas. They also gave us a rundown of the company, and exactly what they expected of us.

A certain man was teaching during the training session. In all of his teaching, he kept saying "It is your attitude, not your aptitude, that determines your altitude". I never heard this saying before. But he said that so many times, I had it memorized by the time the session was finished.

At the close of the training session they had a question and answer period. Several people asked questions. Finally, they released us from the meeting, saying that if anyone has any more questions, we should feel free to call.

On the way home I thought of a question that I didn't think of in the meeting - Are there any quotas to meet? Do they have a minimum performance standard that must be met?

I called them. The lady at the desk answered. I explained to her that I had just come from the meeting and that I have an additional question. She passed the phone to the man who did the presentation.

"Are there any quotas in sales that we have to meet?", I asked.

The man answered, "I told you that it's your attitude, not your aptitude that determines your altitude. Don't bother coming back!" and he hung up!

Such a response tempted me to just get angry, but I realized that no matter how angry I got with that man, it wouldn't do any good. So, instead of getting angry I decided to count this as a learning experience.

Your attitude IS a very significant factor to success in court. You must have the right attitude. The "right attitude" is evident in your character - how we respond to inflammatory remarks, false accusations, and frustrations from the other party, and more importantly, how we respond to the judge.

A good attitude goes deeper than trying to keep it positive. It's all about character.

The "right attitude" can be defined as an attitude of humility, respect, honor, and grace. This differs from a simple "positive attitude" in that it's roots go much deeper. It draws from the wells of wisdom, and grace. How do you respond when you are under tremendous pressure?

The Right Attitude

What does it mean to have the right attitude?

Refuse To Be Baited By Anybody

It is a common occurrence in family court for the opposing party to be purposefully offensive. They know how to push all the right (wrong) buttons. Their strategy is to get you so angry that you blow it! And if you blow it, you risk losing the whole case. They want you to lose it in court. They want to confuse, humiliate, and anger you. But with the right attitude, all of the filth they throw at you will not stick. You have to be a "non-stick" man.

Stay above them. Refuse to be offended. Defend yourself, but not with anger. Stay cool. Answer with matter-of-fact answers that can be proven.

Or, if you cannot say anything that you can prove to be correct, at least answer with a defense that cannot be disproven. Choose to rise higher than the dirty games they play.

Stay Humble

(a) learn how to say "I don't know". If you are asked a question that you don't know the answer to, tell them plainly that you don't know. A lot of people don't know how to say "I don't know".
Pretending like you know something when you really don't will destroy your credibility. And your credibility is your greatest asset in court. Be honest. If you don't know, just say "I don't know". Know when you don't know. And don't be afraid to admit it.

(b) if you don't understand the question, tell them plainly that you don't understand. Once again, it is important to prove yourself to be honest and credible. If you do not fully understand a question, or a request, say so (with an apology).

(c) learn how to admit your shortcomings, and your mistakes. But always end on a positive note. For example, lets say you are accused of having an anger problem. Admit it, but tell the court that you are getting help. Be prepared to prove it, if it is disputed.

Make Peace Whenever Possible

Stay focused on making peace, and not war.

"Making peace" does not mean giving up custody of the child when you know it is not in the child's best interest.

Making peace is not surrendering your child to sub-satisfactory conditions.

Making peace is not surrendering your right to be a parent to your child. Rather, making peace is about the way you "fight".

To make peace is to strategically fight with the right attitude, in the right way, for the right motives - for the best interest of the child.

Show yourself to be a man of peace, reasonable, humble, and respectable.

Know when to compromise, and when not to. Be reasonable, while not compromising the child's best interest. Some things are simply not worth fighting over. Some things do not affect the best interest of the child. Don't get caught up in a war over little things. Don't sweat the small stuff.

Make peace with your ex and do it well - it is the dream of your child.

A Better Way to "Fight" - Focusing on the Positive

Don't go into court with the primary objective being to prove your ex-wife to be an unfit parent. Sure, that can be one of your points. But don't make it your primary point. Don't dwell on the negative.

Your primary objective should be to show the court how it is in the child's best interest to be in your custody. Sell yourself. Sell your home and family environment. And make sure you use <u>at least</u> 2 witnesses to back you up. You cannot go into court alone. You cannot go to court with only witnesses against your ex. The judge needs to see how you, and your home environment is the most stable, secure, safe, and best environment to foster the healthy development of the child.

In other words, "fight" by showing the court who is the best. Don't fight by showing the court who is the worst.

Getting Ready

Men vs. Women in Court

As much as some like to enforce the ideology of equality between sexes, men don't have the same support network as women do.

Even though by law, courts are supposed to treat both sexes the same, there are subtle differences in the way men and women are treated in court. Keep that in mind.

Don't Be Afraid to Ask for Help

As a father, you need all the help you can get! Do not be too proud to ask for help!

Steve Jobs is considered one of the most successful men in the history of electronics and technology. When asked what is the secret to success, Jobs said that the ability to ask for help is a key factor.

Men are notorious for not asking for directions. This is not a good thing - especially when the truth is that fathers going through the family court system need help. Ask!

Don't Worry. It's Normal.

Accept the fact that the following scenarios are the "norm". It is not just happening to you. And realize in the heat of the battle that the judge knows that. Don't panic. Just be prepared.

Scenario #1: No Lawyer

Most fathers cannot afford to go through family court far enough to serve their children justice without running out of finances due to mounting legal fees.
Government programs that fund your legal services can easily be exhausted in a trial. And you will be left without a lawyer to represent you in the heat of the battle.
Know that things are going to move right along with, or without a lawyer.

Scenario #2: Getting emotionally assaulted, and insulted

Family court is not necessarily the most friendly place. Defamation of character is illegal everywhere except in a courtroom. Normally, in a trial, the opposing party can defame, and slander you as much as he/she wants without legal ramifications. You become an open target that gets shot at!
Having said that, be prepared for a nasty fight. Be prepared for an emotional and verbal assault. But keep cool. Do not return an insult for an insult. You must "play" at a higher level.

Scenario #3: False accusations

Be prepared for accusations that are completely false. Learn how to think like the opposing party.
Be prepared for accusations that are "off the wall".

Be prepared to witness your ex acting in a way that you never experienced before.

Be prepared to address any, and every false accusation and call it what it is - false, without credible evidence. Challenge every false accusation.

But always stay cool, and stick to the facts.

The Strategy

Sitting in on a Family Court Trial

There is a lot of "game playing" in family court. As in any game, you have to know the rules. You have to know the "game". And you have to get familiar with the "game" in order to be successful.

You cannot know the "game" without ever seeing it being played. Knowing the rules of the game, and the object of the game won't cut it. You need to see the game played.

Go into family court, sit in on a family trial, and see what goes on. Get to know the judges and the lawyers.

Watching the action in family court is a must! It is the **primary strategy to success**. Observe family court proceedings. Know your court! Know where the parking lot is!

In family court, you are essentially making a "sales pitch". You need to learn how to be effective in producing the evidence. You need to know how to effectively make arguments to support your claims, and your requests in court.

If you are going to play, you must play well. You can't expect to play baseball very well if you never saw a baseball game before. You need to get familiar with the game. <u>Watch the action before you join the action.</u>

How to Sit in on a Family Court Trial

Call the court, ask to speak with the trial coordinator. Ask when the next family court trial is on. Go, and sit in on the trial. In most circumstances, a family court trial is open to the public!

Also there are "open-motion hearings". This is when motions are brought before the court and the public is welcome to sit in on these hearings. Go in, and sit down. Watch the action.

While you are sitting in on a family trial, most likely someone will ask why you are there. Let them know that you are there so that you can learn and observe - so that you don't waste the court's time when the day comes for your proceedings. Or you can just simply say, "I'm just here to observe."

The reason they ask is to find out if you are going to be a witness to one of the parties. Usually, witnesses who are called to testify are not allowed to sit in on the trial. Witnesses are only allowed in the court to testify. But generally speaking, court trials are open to the public.

Go and sit in on as many family court trials as possible! You are going to see why people lose. You are also going to see why people win.

Consider it a **primary part of your training, preparation, and educational experience.**

When it is your turn to stand in front of the judge, that is not the time to be learning. That is when it is the time to apply what you have already learned.

Learn your courthouse from top to bottom. Temper your sales pitch to the judge, if you can.

Sitting in on a trial or court hearings will teach you what distinguishes fathers who win from fathers who lose.

You have to be objective. You have to look at everything from an objective point of view.

Map to Success

You must recognize where you are in the process. If you don't know where you are, then you wouldn't be able to map out where you are going. You are "on the map". But the first thing you must establish when looking at a map is where you are. If you don't know where you are, how can you know how to get to where you want to go?

For example, don't try to present all your evidence and witnesses at the case conference. Knowing where you are in the process helps you become more relaxed, and confident. But it also helps you plan your route to success. You need to know where you are going, and how to get there. Don't treat a settlement conference like a trial!

If you don't know where you are going, then you will probably end up where you don't want to be.

Ask yourself questions like: Where am I in the process? Where am I in the big picture? How can I prepare for the next step? How can I prepare for the ultimate goal - success?

Know and believe that winning = the best interest of your child.

Find a Mentor

It is a good idea to have a mentor to help you through this difficult time. A mentor should be someone who has a good head on their shoulders... someone you can bounce ideas off of, and brainstorm with - someone to help you strategize.

Whatever the case, DO NOT find someone to just complain to. Fathers who are going through family court should not be mere complainers - unless it is with resolve.

In other words, you need to DO SOMETHING about it. Don't just complain. Do something positive to resolve the problem.

Having said that, having a wise, experienced "father" who can give you some solid advice is a true asset.

Biting the Bullet

You must have the ability to "bite the bullet" and spit it back out again gracefully. This is a skill that is priceless. You will be fired at. But you must remain calm, and cool. You must remain on top of everything. Don't take offense easily. Taking offence, and getting angry is just going to drain you of much needed resources to fight the battle, and mar your image in court.

Often, the other party is going to push all the right buttons to get you raging mad. Understand that this is just a tactic to get you to "blow it" in court. Show the court that you are strong, and stable, and not easily angered. This will help your image in the judge's eyes.

Understand that fathers all over the world are going through what you are going through. You are not alone.

Winning is Within Reach

Most of all, you must believe that you **CAN** win. And the truth is - you can! If I can win, so can you! But it is going to take time. And it is going to take a lot of work.

Take the opportunity to prepare while waiting for court. But do whatever you can to make sure that the court proceedings are not put off too long. If you are faced with another party trying to put things off, explain to the judge how putting it off too long can negatively affect the child.
Putting things off too long can work against you, especially if you don't presently have your child with you.

47

But sometimes a delay is inevitable. Look for every opportunity to make the circumstances work for you. Be positive. If there is an inevitable delay in court, see it as a chance to get better prepared.

Parenting Classes

You may want to consider taking parenting classes. This could help you to get insights into the needs of your child at any specific time in their life.

The more information you have, the better informed you are, and the more you can help your child. Consider consulting a professional developmental psychologist.

Draw a Parenting Plan

This is a very important step in the process of preparation. The court needs to see a clear picture of what the child's life would be like in your custody. You need to provide a daily, weekly, and yearly plan. You must show the judge that you have a clear plan for the child.

Make up a schedule of what the child's daily life would look like if the child was in your custody.

Some of the things to consider when drawing up a parenting plan:
* What time would the child get up in the morning?
* When is breakfast?
* Would the child go to school? If so, what time? How would the child get to school? And how would the child get home from school?
* What are the mealtimes?
* What are the recreational times?
* Where in the schedule does the child have "quality time" to bond with you and the rest of your family?
* When is bedtime?
* Special events?
* Family trips?
* Annual family traditions?
* Vacations?

Think about what goes on in your child's world from their perspective. What would it be like to be your child? What kind of home environment would you like? What kind of schedule would you like? What would you like to do? Where would you like to go?

It is very important that you are well prepared. It is very possible that you can out-prepare your ex and her lawyer!

Some lawyers are lazy. They don't prepare very well. And if you are representing yourself, chances are they will prepare even less. They expect you to be like everyone else who is self-represented - ignorant, and ill-prepared. They think that you are easy to defeat. Surprise the opposing lawyer with your knowledge, and preparation. And chances are - You will win! It doesn't take a law degree.

Be well prepared. Know enough procedure to get the job done, you will probably do a better job than a lawyer because you know the facts better than anybody. And you are more passionate about it than anybody else.

How to Research

Every country, and every jurisdiction differs. You must do your research.

Here are some helpful tips:

The Internet

We have a tool that is indispensable: the Internet. The first thing you need to do is find information about your local court system, and applicable laws in your area. Every jurisdiction is different. You need to find information specific to your area. Find out what court you will be dealing with if you don't already know. Then, go to the Internet for information about that court. If you don't already have the contact information, you should find the address, and phone numbers.

You must also find out what legislation applies to your jurisdiction. The Internet is a great source of information. Make sure you are downloading information specific to your region.
Look for laws, and "acts" that are applicable to your case.

Also, search the Internet for tutorials, tips, and advice pertaining to family court, court procedures, and trials. You should be able to find a substantial amount of information about how to prepare your opening and closing statements, as well as how to perform a cross-examination, and so on...

Court Clerks

Call the court and ask where you can get more information. Is there any free legal help that you can get? Ask them if you can download court forms from the Internet. Ask them about where you can get more help.

Ask the court clerk for assistance whenever needed. Court clerks do not provide "legal advice", although they may be able to help with procedural matters. They can help you by guiding you to the right forms and paperwork to fill out. They can also help you by telling you where you are in the process.

Go to the court website applicable to your location. You will most likely find court forms to download, as well as a "self help" guide. You may also find a lot of information about the court process. It is imperative that you find out all that you can about your court, it's rules and procedures.

You may also want to look into case law. Most lawyers refer to previous court cases when duking it out in court. Once again, there should be a website where you can research case law in your area.

Q&A

"Do I need an attorney or can I represent myself?"

Most fathers that go to trial end up unrepresented. You have the right to represent yourself if you choose. However, self-representation is not the "best case scenario" in the eyes of the court, and you should acknowledge that.

During trial, one of the first things you should say in your opening statement is "Your Honor, first and foremost I want to apologize for not having an attorney. I realize that this is not the best case scenario. However, I am willing to do whatever it takes to co-operate with the court, and make this trial go as smooth as possible. Please accept my apology."

Keep in mind that you do not have to have a lawyer. But, it is in your best interest to have a lawyer as long as possible.

"What if my ex has an attorney and I don't?"

This is what I faced. My ex had an attorney and I did not. After all was said and done, I won. Don't be intimidated. Be cool, confident, and get educated!

"Will the Judge 'look down' on me if I don't have an attorney?"

The judge is not supposed to be biased toward a party that has an attorney. But you must realize that your job is to get educated in legal matters. Make it easy on the judge. Otherwise, if you don't know what you are doing, and/or you are not properly prepared, the judge will not have a good impression of you. This is not the way to obtain victory in family court. You must educate yourself, and you must be prepared.

Do your best to make it as easy as possible for the judge to do his, or her job. If you cause the judge undue problems because of your lack of knowledge, be quick to apologize for the inconvenience.

"Can I go to court and talk to the Judge by myself without the other party present?"

You cannot talk to the judge by yourself unless you file an emergency motion. You can file an emergency motion if you have sufficient evidence to believe that if your ex finds out you are going to court - she will run with the child, or cause the child harm.

In this case, you need to present enough evidence to convince the judge that this may happen, and ask the judge for an order to restrain your ex from leaving the county with the child - or any other action that may have to be enforced to ensure your child's best interest.

Make sure you ask for an order for police enforcement if you foresee your ex not cooperating with the court order. If you don't ask, you probably will not get it. And if you don't have an order for police enforcement, then the police may not be able to help you if your ex does not comply.

"I was just at court, what next?"

Finding out where you are in the process is crucial. You need to talk to your court clerk, or counsel. This process differs throughout the world. You need to ask how many more court hearings you need to attend before trial.
Where I come from, it starts with a motion hearing, then a case conference, then a settlement conference, then a trial management conference, then a trial. But this process can vary, even in my jurisdiction. You need to ask your local court, or a local lawyer about the details that apply to your jurisdiction.

When Things Are Not Going Right

When things are not going right, stop and reassess. Try to look at things from a detached point of view. Step back from yourself and look at it from a stranger's point of view. Ask honest, unbiased people for their honest, unbiased opinions, and advice.

When things aren't working - modify your approach. Note: modify your approach, not your goals. Never give up your goals when you know it is in the best interest of the child.

Tips

* Save all text messages. One way to save a text message is to send it to your email. Try to ensure everything has time stamps, and dates. You may have to ask your cell provider for other ways you can save your text messages.

* The footsteps of a successful father are documentation, documentation and documentation. Always document. Write down everything. Make sure you write down all the details about the event you are documenting. Include dates, times, and every other meaningful detail of interest.

* It is important to know the psychology of the person you are dealing with. Learn how to negotiate.

* Stay around positive people.

* Don't come across as being overly argumentative, or unreasonable. State the facts passionately, but don't let emotions get the best of you.

*Pictures are primary evidence. Take pictures, and lots of pictures. Take pictures of your home, pictures of you spending special time with your child. Use these pictures as proof if there is a dispute about a certain fact you wish to present to the court.

More Do's and Don'ts

Lawyers seem to like to delay. This can work for you if you are not properly prepared, but too much delay can work against you. Move your matter forward vigorously. Don't allow too much delay. It could work against you - especially if your child is not currently residing with you.

Don't be overly provocative or inflammatory. Don't call your ex-wife names. You may think they (your ex, her lawyer, and her witnesses) are evil and vile, but don't say that in an affidavit, or in court. If you do, you are going to be looked at as the war-monger. Just state the facts without getting too personal - even when they do. Show yourself that you are better. Understand that false accusations, reviling, and disrespectful behavior is normal in court.

Rest assured that the judge knows that. Don't get your nose out of joint. Show the judge that you are responsible, reasonable, and no matter how much crap the other party throws on you, it doesn't stick! The judge will be impressed with the integrity of your character.

Respond to false accusations, and false statements with facts. Don't let anger get the best of you. Don't play into the hands of your opponents. Don't give them first-hand evidence that you have an anger problem.

Stay focussed on the goal. If you have been deeply involved with the child from the beginning, that child will have a bond with you.

Court Rules & Procedures

You cannot simply fill out a bunch of papers and file them with the court so that you can tell the judge your side of the story. It doesn't work that way. There is a proper procedure to follow. There are court rules to follow.

You may be able to find basic court rules posted at your local courthouse. You can get a lot of help with procedural matters by asking court clerks. Normally, court clerks will make it very clear that they cannot give you legal advice. But don't let that discourage you from getting "procedural advice" i.e. what forms should I fill out next? How should I prepare my documents? What is a trial record? How should I serve my papers on the other party? etc... etc...
Most of all - be determined.

You must be on top of things. You must know applicable deadlines. There are serious consequences for missing your court date. There are also serious consequences for missing certain deadlines.

Remember while attending court:

* Be prepared.
* Be on Time.
* Know your Family Court rules
* Be courteous and respectful
* Be reasonable
* Dress appropriately
* Speak loud and clear
* Be assertive

Come before the judge with a positive attitude.

Passionate people are persuasive people. Be passionate about your case. Be passionate, but don't let your emotions get the best of you. Don't give the judge first hand evidence why a restraining order is necessary!

Preparing for Court

Keep in mind that there are court fees that apply to certain things like photocopies, filing trial records, etc... If you cannot afford certain fees, you may qualify for a reduction or total coverage of some fees. If you are having a hard time paying the fees, let the court clerk know that you do not have the finances required, and ask your court clerk if you can apply for a reduction in fees.

Rehearse your arguments in front of a mirror and/or with someone who can be a good "devil's advocate".

If you are self-represented, you must handle your family trial from start to finish. Although this may sound daunting, if you are well prepared, and determined to win, you have the upper edge - no matter what anyone says. You can win!
Find a few good proofreaders. Friends and family can make good proofreaders. This is especially needed when you are writing affidavits and other court documents.

Make sure you brainstorm with other people. Have other people act as the devil's advocate. Practice presenting your case. Have a mock trial.

Don't overestimate your ex wife's honesty. Expect her to lie about anything and everything. Expect her to be the person you never knew her to be. Prepare proof for everything you say. Proof can come in the form of documents, affidavits, videos, audio recordings, emails, printouts of social media web sites, and witnesses. Keep in mind that everything said in the witness stand under oath, is considered "evidence".

Witnesses

Use your immediate family as witnesses - after all, this is family court! Your spouse, your siblings, and your parents are an asset to you in family court. Close friends who frequent your home are also a great choice for witnesses.

You need witnesses that frequent your home, or live with you. The judge is looking for witnesses that can testify of the stability of the home, how well you interact with your child, how you help in the child's education, etc…

Does anyone witness you helping your child in his/her education, or homework? Does anyone witness how well you interact with your child in and out of the home?

You need at least two or more witnesses that you know well, and that see you with your child on a regular basis.

Trial Procedure

1. Normally, a trial starts with an *opening statement*. The applicant/plaintiff is the first to make an opening statement, followed by the respondent/defendant.
2. Next, the applicant is called to the stand for a direct examination, followed by a cross examination by the opposing party.
3. Then the applicant's witnesses take the stand. Each one will receive a direct examination from the party they represent, followed by a cross examination by the opposing party.
4. Then the respondent will take the stand. He/she will undergo direct examination, followed by a cross examination by the other party.
5. The respondent's witnesses are called to the stand. They will be given a direct examination by the respondent, followed by a cross-examination by the opposing party.
6. Then the applicant and the respondent will give their *closing statements*.

If you are self-represented you do not give yourself a *direct examination*. Instead, you simply take the stand swear/affirm, then tell your story. Make sure you write it down so that when you are in the stand you simply read it. This enables you to stay focussed.

As a self-represented father, the opposing party will cross-examine you. And you will have to give a direct examination to all your witnesses, and cross examine the other party, and her witnesses.

Opening Statement

In the opening statement, you, or your lawyer, will tell the judge a very brief summary of your case, and what you are asking the court for.

Direct Examination

The first thing you must do when giving your witnesses a direct examination is to identify them, and introduce them to the court. You do this by asking them questions and letting them tell the court. i.e. How old are you? Where do you live? ...etc...

Establish that your witness has personal knowledge of the event in question. Ask your witnesses questions that establish that they are first-hand witness of the events, and circumstances in question.

If you are representing yourself, you will be the one who gives your witnesses a "direct examination", and you will be the one who will be cross examining her witnesses that will be witnessing against you.

When you are giving your own witnesses a "direct examination" you must ask your witnesses "friendly" questions, leading them to testify of the facts you wish to bring before the court. Ask questions to establish that your witnesses are credible, knowledgeable, first hand witnesses of the facts you wish to present. You must learn to ask questions that allow your witness to explain whatever he/she knows that supports your case without putting words into his/her mouth. This is called "leading the witness".

A few examples of "direct examination" questions are:

How often do you come over to my place?
Do you see me interacting with my son?

Explain that.
Where were you on the night of Tuesday, November 26th, 2013?
What time was it?
What did you see?
How long did you stay?
Was the child crying?

Cross Examination

Cross examination of your ex-wife, and her witnesses must be done at a totally different tone. These questions are aggressive, more or less, putting words in the mouths of the witnesses, hoping that they will agree to it. There are many ways to cross-examine someone.

If you have a feeling that a certain witness may be prone to deny they went to the park, don't ask them if they did, ask them why they did it!

An example of a cross examination question would be:

Why did you go to the park to meet with your friends at 10pm, on March 13th, 2013?
Why did you take the child with you?
Isn't it true that you burst out in anger?
Isn't it true that you were out until 2am?

The idea is to make it easy for them to agree to the facts that you wish to present to the court. Try to minimize any opportunity for them to lie. One way to do this is to ask questions that more or less put words in the witnesses mouths, and make it easy for them to agree to it, or admit it in court.

Normally, in a cross examination you try to ask questions that limit the witness's answer to a simple yes, or no. This is in contrast to a direct examination when you open the question up and allow the witness to explain.

Another cross-examination tactic is to try to catch them in a lie. Or try to get them (the other party's witnesses) to contradict one another. If you can get the opposing witnesses to contradict themselves, this destroys their credibility, and the "weight" of their words in court.

Closing Statement

In your closing statement you, or your lawyer will summarize what all the evidence means. Here is when you pull it all together and make a final statement to the court. This is like the final "sales pitch" to the court.
In the closing statement you can also repeat all your requests to the court - custody, support arrears expunged, etc...etc...

Preparing Your Scripts

It is imperative that you script your opening statement, direct, and cross examinations of each witness, and your closing statement. You should write it out.

Don't give these scripts to anyone else. Don't give them to the court. They are only for your eyes to see. And make sure that you leave plenty of room between lines to write notes, as during the trial a lot of things can come up that you did not think about.

You should have all the questions that you wish to use when cross examining your ex-wife - all written out, in an easy to read, easy to follow format. You need to leave plenty of space in between each question for room to take notes during trial.

Suppose you are listening to her testimony on the stand. She is telling the court her side of the story. She says something that you didn't expect her to say, but you know that you can cross-examine her on that quite effectively. You sit there, with a pen in your hand, ready to write more questions on your "cross examination" script. You add notes to your already prepared cross-examination script.

This way, you don't miss a beat. When you are called to cross examine her, you have everything ready. You have all your "ducks in a row". You don't miss anything. You are organized.

The same goes for her witnesses. You should already know who is going to be on the stand well before the trial. This way you can prepare your cross-examination of the them - assuming you know who they are, you may have a good idea of what they are going to say.

If she brings witnesses into trial without giving you adequate notice beforehand - witnesses that you are not expecting, you should tell the judge that you were not informed about the inclusion of these witnesses. Therefore, the judge should either exclude them from the trial, or postpone the trial to give you extra time to prepare to cross-examine these witnesses.

You should prepare cross-examination questions for each witness that she has. You should have a different set of questions for each witness.

Once again, while they are up testifying against you, you should have your cross-examination script in front of you - the one that you tailored specifically for that witness. As that witness is talking, perhaps they bring up some things you didn't expect. You leave enough room in between questions to write down additional questions on the spur-of-the-moment.
This way, you stay on top of things. You stay organized. And you don't miss a beat.

What is a Motion?

In its simplest definition, a motion is a request to the judge. More specifically, a motion is a procedural matter that brings an issue before the court for a decision.

Motions may be made at any point in the proceedings, although that right is regulated by court rules which can vary in different jurisdictions.

The party requesting the motion is called the *movant*, or the *moving party*. The party opposing the motion is the *nonmovant* or the *nonmoving party*.

A motion can be made orally, while you are before the judge, especially during a hearing, conference, or trial.

A motion can also be made in written form, by filing a motion in court. Usually, a court case begins by a written motion that is filed in court.

Motions, especially in written form, are often accompanied by an affidavit to support that motion.

Filing a motion in court is a way to begin a court case. Search the Internet for the applicable website of your court or jurisdiction. You should find downloadable, and printable motion forms there. You may want to call the local court and ask the court clerk for assistance in finding such forms.

Filing a motion can be as simple as filling out a few forms and taking them to your local courthouse. Sometimes motions need to be "served" upon the other party. Ask your court clerks for details on how to file a motion specific to your case.

What is an Affidavit

An affidavit is a written sworn statement of fact voluntarily made by an *affiant* or *deponent* under an oath, or affirmation administered by a person authorized to do so by law. An affidavit is witnessed as to the authenticity of the affiant's signature by a taker of oaths, such as a notary public or commissioner of oaths.

An affidavit is a type of verified statement taken under oath or penalty of perjury, and this serves as evidence to its veracity and is required for court.

In simple terms, an affidavit is a document that is sworn under oath, and signed in the presence of an authorized witness.

How to Write an Affidavit

An affidavit usually includes an account of some aspect of the case. Affidavits are a very important part of a case. When you start a case, usually an affidavit is filed with a motion, in support of that motion.

In writing an affidavit, you must divide your statement, or your testimony into separate <u>numbered paragraphs</u>. Each paragraph represents a single fact, point, idea, or topic.

For example, if you have 3 facts that you wish to present in an affidavit, you should have 3 numbered paragraphs, each paragraph corresponding to a separate fact.

Try to be as clear and concise as possible when writing your affidavit. Include names, addresses, and dates whenever possible. When referring to your child, including the child's full name and date of birth.

You can refer to other documents, and photographs in your affidavit. But if you do, make sure that you attach them to your affidavit, and label each document "Exhibit A", "Exhibit B"... etc...etc...

You don't have to use a letter-naming system. You can also label them as "Exhibit 1", "Exhibit 2", etc...

Make sure you attach these documents or photographs to your affidavit, and make sure you have each document clearly labeled accordingly.

For example, if you want to refer to a photograph, you can call the photograph, "Exhibit A", and then make sure you attach the photograph to the affidavit, and clearly label it, "Exhibit A"

Corresponding With the Judge

In communicating with the judge, you must be respectful. You must follow court rules, and you must show yourself to be in submission to the court in all things, and at all times.

There may be times when the judge may not make the right calls. In such cases, you must use utmost discretion. There is a thing they call "respectful pushback".

"Respectful pushback" is when you openly, but carefully, and respectfully disagree with the judge.

Always address the judge appropriately. Typically, you must address the judge as "Your Honor". Also, be sure to stand when speaking to the judge. If in doubt, check with the clerks at your local courthouse about the proper way to address the judge.

How to Argue

Sometimes, choosing not to argue is in fact the way to win. This is especially true in personal relationships.

But in court, if you do not argue, you lose. If your wife said that you assaulted her, and you don't argue against that, then all the advantage will be given to your wife, and what she says will be assumed as truth.

Arguing effectively is a learned skill. You must be able to present your argument in a way that's effective. Here are a few pointers to consider:

Don't let your tongue get away on you! Don't say too much. Think ahead - if I say this, she will probably say that.

Learn how to control what you say. Develop this skill by mock-arguments. Rehearse your arguments, and be the "devil's advocate". Think of any and every way that argument can be opposed; thus minimize the damage by learning how to avoid opening the "can worms".

When arguing, you must be willing to listen to your opposition. You must learn how to listen first, then speak. You don't have to agree, but only listen. Try to present your argument in a way that your audience (the judge) wants to hear it. Be respectful. **Be courteous to the opposing party, regardless of how they are treating you. Do not return insult for insult.**

Show respect for the other party's arguments against you. Suppose her lawyer quotes a previous court case to reinforce his argument. You should start your argument by saying, "I appreciate what Mr. Smith (opposing lawyer) said about "doe vs henry", but I do not believe that applies in my case because...."

Notice the respectful, and courteous tone. Stay positive, respectful, and courteous. Don't let your emotions get the best of you.

Be passionate, but don't be overly emotional. Passionate arguments are compelling and persuasive. Show the judge that you really believe in what you are saying. Speak loud and clear, but don't be irritating. Be persuasive. Take the judge "by the hand", so speak, and lead him/her down the path of truth. If there is any dispute about what you say, make sure you can back that up with documents, or photographs. Always have proof.

Be confident, but don't be arrogant. No one likes an arrogant man. Don't be caught up in your own rhetoric. Be real.

In Trial

Dressing for Court

You should dress respectfully, but don't go to court overdressed. You don't want to present yourself looking too "cheesy". Don't dress casual either, as it shows lack of respect. If in doubt, it is better to be a tad bit overdressed, as opposed to being a tad bit underdressed.

Make sure you show up early. Showing up at court early gives you an advantage. You can take some time to settle in. This can help take the "edge" off.

Furthermore, being there early also gives you a chance to speak with other party's lawyer. Use this to your advantage. The more you hear about what they have to say in advance, the longer you can think about it, and plan a good rebuttal.

Make sure you take two working pens and a writing pad. You will need to take notes - and lots of them. You don't want to have to ask the judge for a pen!

Make sure you have at least three copies of every document. One copy for the judge, one of the other party, and one for yourself. You don't want the judge to dismiss the court just because you are not properly prepared.

Know when to sit down and shut up. Don't ramble any more than you have to.

Don't try too hard to impress the judge. Most judges will be able to see right through that. Be real, honest, and helpful to the judge by providing relevant information.

If you don't understand what is being said, apologize for not understanding, and ask the judge to rephrase it. Likewise if you don't hear something that is said in court, kindly ask the judge, lawyer, or person to repeat.

Do not interrupt the judge - EVER - even if the judge interrupts you, don't interrupt the judge. Give the judge time to say everything he or she wants to say without interruption.

It is always best to settle things out of court, before a trial. But don't give up your right to be a parent. And don't give up your fight for custody, if in fact it is in the best interest of the child.

Always refer to your child as "our child", **not** "my child"

Don't say, "my son".

Say, "our son".

Know that the number one objective of the opposing party is to discredit you by proving that your testimony is untrue, or invalid. You need to be assertive - but not rude. Having your papers in order and a brief outline in front of you can give you confidence.

Stay calm while under attack. Develop the ability to see things from the perspective of your adversary, while conforming to the "rules of the game".

Make sure that you can back up everything you say in court. Make sure that you know what you are talking about. And most of all, make sure that you know what you don't know. In other words, you must first be honest with yourself. You must first be able to differentiate truth from fiction. You must be able to step out of yourself and view things from the outside.

Believe that the judge WANTS to rule in your favor. But you must give the judge the power to do so by your evidence. You must give the judge the evidence that he, or she needs to justify his, or her decision.

Show the judge what you are doing to minimize the trauma of the court battle on the child. Show the judge what you are doing to keep the child away from the conflict between you and your ex, and the stress of the legal proceedings.

You must convince the judge that the time you wish to spend with your child is of great benefit to the child. The court's focus is supposed to be on the best interest of the child. If you are both fighting, how is that good for the child? Show the judge that you are willing to make peace with your ex whenever possible.

A mature person takes responsibility for their part in the problem. Show the judge who the mature person is! If you have done something wrong, and it is proven in court, then show the judge that you are willing to do whatever it takes to solve it.

Don't bore the judge - get his attention and keep his attention.

Stress Management

In order to bare stress effectively you must be emotionally, and physically healthy. Make sure you engage in physical exercise, eat right, and make sure you get a good night's sleep.

Winners vs. Losers

Losers usually don't have much of a support network. You need a strong support network - friends, family, extended family, etc...

Choose your friends wisely. Choosing the wrong friends can cost you everything.

Winners recognize the "fog" of divorce. They recognize and realize how their judgement can get distorted, or impaired in times of stress. Be honest with yourself, and with others. Do not deny reality. Be humble. Be real.

Get into a Support Group

Being in a group setting is very important. It tends to add another dimension. One-on-one usually doesn't do it. But being in a room full of fathers going through what you are can be very supportive, educational, and enlightening. Do whatever you can to find a local fathers support group.
Attend as much as you can. Ask questions, and get involved. Some of the best advice you can get is from fathers who have already "been there, done that" and won!

The Trial is Over. Now What?

After your trial is finished, it is up to the judge to make a verdict, aka "judgement", or "endorsement". The timing of this is entirely up to the judge. It could take hours. It could take months. It all depends on the circumstances. If the judge believes your matter needs to be dealt with immediately, you may see an answer quickly. If the judge does not see an urgency to your case, it could take months.

When the judgement is in, it needs to be made into a court order. Making a judgement into a court order is a matter of copying the keys points from the judgement to a court order form. If you are self-represented and you won your case, it is your responsibility to ensure the endorsement from the judge gets made into a court order. Check with your lawyer or your court clerk about the details as each courthouse and each jurisdiction can be different.

When you do hear back from the judge, it is important to minimize stress and trauma in the life of the child. If the judgement calls for a major change in the life of the child, you need to make sure the transition is as smooth as possible.

If you lose your case, don't despair! Remember, I lost the first time around. Custody is always on the table. Even though a court order may be "Final", it is not permanent. Circumstances can change. Never give up. Never give up your right, and privilege to parent your child. Next time around you can win just as I did.

If you "won" your case, you will probably get some kickback from your ex. Same rules apply out of court, as in court in this regard. Stay calm. Proceed to enforce the judgement effectively. Make sure the court order is made. If there are any violations of that court order, you may want to file a notice of contempt motion.

Through it all, don't belittle, or diss your ex in front of your child. Keep the child out of the "heat of the battle". Be sensitive to the child's needs and emotional well-being. Be the best parent you can be. Be a good example to your child.

The bottom line is always the best interest of the child.

For speaking engagements contact:

csummerhayes@gmail.com

www.ingramcontent.com/pod-product-compliance
Lightning Source LLC
Chambersburg PA
CBHW071306170526
45165CB00003B/1439